It's Raining Cats and Dogs

CHATHAM RIVER PRESS
New York

DEC 1990

Created and manufactured by arrangement with Ottenheimer Publishers, Inc.
Copyright © 1990 Ottenheimer Publishers, Inc.
This 1990 edition published by Chatham River Press,
distributed by Crown Publishers, Inc., 225 Park Avenue South,
New York, New York 10003
Printed in Singapore
ISBN 0-517-68882-4
h g f e d c b a

Introduction

This book is filled with idioms, the phrases, or groups of words, that make our language more exciting. Some of them you may already know and even use! Others may be new to you and may seem rather strange! Each of these phrases has a special meaning, a meaning that is unexpected. This is what makes it an idiom. You may know what each word of an idiom means by itself, but still not understand exactly what the phrase means!

Have you ever heard someone say "It's raining cats and dogs"? Maybe you've said it yourself. You know that there really aren't cats and dogs falling from the sky, so why would someone say that? Using this idiom puts a little excitement in a weather report. It's a colorful way to say it's raining very hard! If you didn't know what the phrase meant, would it help you to look up each word in the dictionary? No! Instead you would have to ask someone what it means or use this book to learn its special meaning.

In case you're curious about the idiom, "It's raining cats and dogs," you'll be surprised to learn that people have been saying it for more than 300 years. People may have started saying this because the thunder and lightning in a rainstorm sound like a cat and dog fighting. Or it might have begun to be used in the days when people thought cats could make it storm and dogs could make the wind blow.

Here is an example of how you might use this idiom: Imagine that you are talking to your friend on the telephone. Suddenly it starts raining so hard that you can't see the tree in your front yard. You say, "Is it storming at your house? It's raining cats and dogs here!"

This book will explain many more idioms to you. It tells you what they mean, how they are used, how they became part of our language and how *you* can use them.

It's Raining Cats and Dogs presents 38 idioms that make our language colorful, interesting, and ever-changing.

Learning more about idioms may help you be *"On the nose"* when you want to *"Pull the wool over someone's eyes!"*

THROW IN THE TOWEL

When you *throw in the towel*, you quit! You surrender! You know that you can't keep on going so you give up before the end.

This saying comes from the boxing ring where managers use towels to dry off the boxers between rounds. A boxing match is supposed to last ten rounds. But if one of the boxers is hurt, his manager knows it's time to stop the fight. Since he won't be needing the towel anymore, he throws it into the ring.

Imagine that you and two of your friends are building a treehouse. They want it to have windows, but you don't. After trying to get them to change their minds, you finally *throw in the towel* and help them to cut out the windows.

SOUR GRAPES

Sour grapes are not something to eat! *Sour grapes* means saying you didn't want something just because you didn't get it. It's also saying something nasty or negative about that thing.

The first one to have *sour grapes* was a fox! In Aesop's Fables, which are very old stories that teach us lessons, a fox jumps up and tries to get a delicious-looking bunch of grapes over 100 times! Finally he is so tired, he gives up. He walks off, grumbling to himself, "Nasty, sour things, I know you are not fit at all for a gentleman's eating!"

Imagine that you and a friend see another friend on his new silver and red dirt bike. Your friend says he thinks it's an ugly bike. You know that's *sour grapes* for just yesterday he said he wished he had that same kind of bike!

SELL LIKE HOTCAKES

Peanuts! Popcorn! Cotton candy! These are some of the delicious foods you might buy at a fair today. Have you ever thought, "I can't wait to get to the fair to buy some hotcakes?" Probably not! But, believe it or not, for children 100 years ago hotcakes or pancakes were a favorite treat at fairs! And because hotcakes were so popular and sold so well, people started saying that anything that sold quickly *sold like hotcakes*!

Imagine that you and a friend have set up a lemonade stand. After your first pitcher is gone, you run into your house and call, "Mom! Can you please make some more lemonade? It's *selling like hotcakes*!"

I'LL EAT MY HAT

What are your favorite things to eat? Chicken? Bananas? Cheese? Your hat? Not many people would really want to eat their hats. But a lot of people say, *"I'll eat my hat!"* If someone is so sure that what he is saying is right, he will offer to eat his hat if he is wrong because he is confident that he won't have to swallow his hat. A bird watcher might say, "That's a redheaded woodpecker or *"I'll eat my hat!"*

Imagine that you and a friend are at the circus. You look over and see your teacher in the popcorn line. Your friend doesn't believe that your teacher is there. You are so sure that you say, "That is Mr. Palmer or *I'll eat my hat!*"

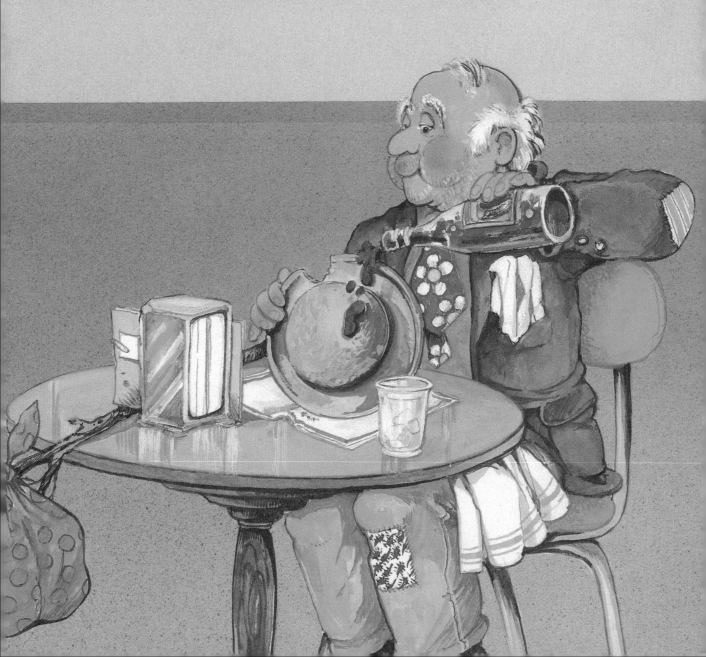

TURN OVER A NEW LEAF

No matter where you are, you can *turn over a new leaf*. You can be in a forest or in the middle of a desert! You can be in a park or on top of a very high building! The only thing you don't need in order to *turn over a new leaf* is. . . a leaf!

When you decide to change your ways or to start over again, you are *turning over a new leaf*. We use this expression because when people are making plans they often write them on paper. A sheet of paper is sometimes called a "folio." Folio means "a leaf." When we are writing our plans for a fresh start, we turn over a new "folio" or leaf to write on.

Imagine that everyone knows you don't like to eat vegetables. But one night at dinner you help yourself to *both* green beans and carrots! Your parents look as if they can't believe their eyes! You happily announce, "I'm *turning over a new leaf*!"

ANTS IN YOUR PANTS

Have you ever looked closely at an ant hill or watched the ants in an ant farm? Ants always seem to be busy! They move quickly from one place to another carrying bits of food, sticks, or even other ants.

There are also other little living things that move around a lot—children! Teachers and parents are always wondering why some children are so squirmy. Sometimes the grownups like to tease the children and ask them, "Do you have *ants in your pants?*" This usually makes the children laugh and move around even more! How would you feel if you had *ants in your pants*?

Imagine that you have gone to a puppet show with your grandmother. First you sit in your seat. Then you sit on her lap. Then you sit on your knees. Finally your grandmother hugs you and whispers, "Do you have *ants in your pants?*" You both giggle and watch the rest of the show!

MONEY DOESN'T GROW ON TREES

This reminds us that money isn't something that we can continually keep getting more and more of! Sometimes it is hard to get more! Sometimes we can't get any more unless we work for it.

Imagine that you and your brother each receive one dollar from your favorite aunt. Your brother goes to the store, spends all of his money, and asks for more. You say to him, "You should think before you spend all of your money. *Money doesn't grow on trees*, you know!"

A BED OF ROSES

When you are on *a bed of roses*, you are feeling very happy!

A rose is a special flower. We give a rose or roses to people to show that we really care about them. Roses are used at special times. People throw rose petals at brides and grooms. An actress gets roses at the end of a play, an ice skater at the end of a performance.

The Romans filled their mattresses with rose petals. How lovely that must have smelled!

Imagine that your sister got a great mark on her book report *and* won a chess game. She is so happy! She is on *a bed of roses*!

ALL THUMBS

Your thumb is an important part of your hand. It helps you hold a book, or a needle, or a baseball bat. But what do you think would happen if you had ten thumbs and no fingers? Suddenly you would be very clumsy! It would be hard for you to draw or dress a doll, because it's your fingers that help you make these small movements. That's why when people say, "He's all thumbs," they mean someone is clumsy.

Imagine that your cousin who is a football player on his school team comes to visit you. After you play football together you ask him for help with your new space shuttle model. He laughs and says, "You wouldn't want my help! With anything smaller than a football, I'm all thumbs!"

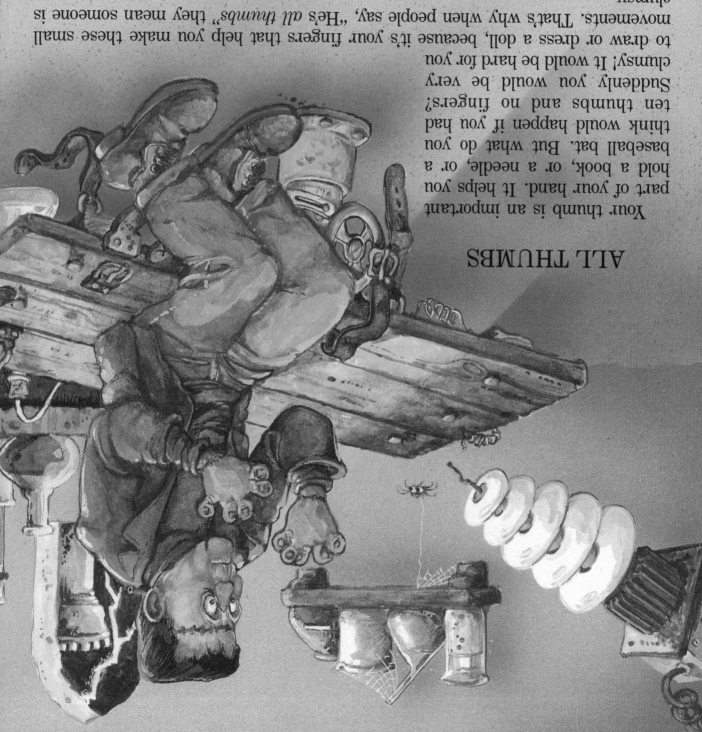

CRYING CROCODILE TEARS

Crocodiles and people have never really been friends. But a crocodile loves to meet people—especially when it is hungry and the people get too close! People used to think that crocodiles cried while they happily ate their victims!!

We know crocodiles don't really cry. But we sometimes say a person is *crying crocodile tears*. That doesn't mean she has little crocodiles rolling down her cheeks! It means that she is only pretending to be sad. Sometimes people *cry crocodile tears* when they want everyone to think they are sorry for doing something wrong when they aren't really sad at all!

Imagine that you have saved the very last piece of your birthday cake to have for a bedtime snack. When you catch your brother eating it, he thinks it's funny and starts laughing. But as soon as your mom comes in the kitchen, he starts crying and acting like he's sorry. You tell your mom, "Don't be fooled. He's *crying crocodile tears!*"

BEAT THE BAND

Bang! Bang! Rat-a-tat-tat! bangs the drum. Boom! Boom! booms the tuba.
Tweet! Tweet! tweets the flute. Flags wave and people cheer as the band plays at the
Fourth of July concert! Bands have been an exciting and loud part of celebrations for
a long time! Nothing stands out more than the band. There might be singing and
dancing, but nothing can beat the band!

Today we say that something *beats the band* only if it is very fast or noisy or is
outstanding in some way.

Imagine that it is your final race at your school's spring
track day. You really want to win the blue ribbon. As you
cross the finish line you look up to see your friends cheering
and clapping to *beat the band!*

JUMP ON THE BANDWAGON

One hundred years ago, in many countries, but especially in the United States, wagons with lively musical bands moved through the streets in order to get people's attention. These wagons were called bandwagons. A person who wanted to be elected mayor would use a bandwagon to get people to come and hear him or her speak. People who liked the candidate would actually *jump up on the bandwagon* to show their support.

Today we say people *jump on the bandwagon* when they support a new idea that looks like it will be a big success or be very popular.

Imagine that some of your friends have started wearing red high top shoes to school every day. You think, "I'm going to *jump on the bandwagon* and wear my red high tops, too!"

BREAK THE ICE

When water freezes and ships can't get to their ports, sometimes they must wait until the ice melts. Other times special ice-breaking boats clear a path for them to get through.

When we speak of *breaking the ice*, it can be winter *or* summer! Sometimes when we meet someone new we can't think of anything to say. We get stuck like the ships in the ice. Just as the boat clears a path, we try to think of something to say or do to start a conversation. For example: playing games at parties often makes strangers laugh and talk with one another. Games are a good way to *break the ice.*

Imagine that you just met a new boy at school. You really like him but you don't know what to say to him. Then you see he's carrying a book called *Creepy Crawly Insects.* You think, "We both like reading about insects. Maybe I'll show him the spider I caught yesterday. That should *break the ice!*"

PULLING YOUR LEG

Has anyone ever told you a story so exciting that your eyes get bigger and your mouth drops open? Maybe your Aunt Sue tells you she once wrestled a bear for an hour! Just as you move to the edge of your seat waiting to hear more, she laughs and says, "I'm just *pulling your leg*!" When people say they're *pulling your leg*, they mean they are teasing or fooling you!

Imagine that you are telling your friend about a fish you caught. Because he's so interested, you keep adding more to the story! "SNAP! A fish got a hold of my line. It was so strong it pulled our boat out to the middle of the lake!" Just as you get to the part where this giant fish bites your boat in two, you laugh and say, "Im just *pulling your leg*! The fish was really only six inches long!"

BEAT AROUND THE BUSH

You've probably never seen anyone hitting a bush, but long ago, bird hunters would *beat around bushes* to scare the birds hiding there. When the birds flew up, the hunters would aim and shoot. Today, when someone is *beating around the bush*, it means that he is not directly answering the question—instead of hitting the bird first, he is circling the bush!

Imagine that your sister asks if she can borrow your soccer ball. You tell her about all the goals you scored with it and how she can be a better soccer player. After listening to you for ten minutes, she says, "Please quit *beating around the bush*! Just tell me yes or no!"

A STICK IN THE MUD

If someone says, "He's *a stick in the mud*," you probably picture a person looking like a stick stuck in the mud. But what is really stuck is that person's mind. He doesn't want to try anything new; he is "stuck" in his ways.

In the days when people rode in horse-drawn wagons on dirt roads, sometimes the wheels would get stuck in the mud. It was hard to move the wagon—just like it's hard to get someone who is *a stick in the mud* to try a new idea!

Imagine that you and a friend are exploring the woods behind your house. You always take the path around the fallen tree, but today you want to follow the creek. Your friend insists that you go the old way. You say to him, "Don't be such *a stick in the mud*!"

BURY YOUR HEAD IN THE SAND

When someone says, "You can't just *bury your head in the sand*," do you look at her strangely? Do you look around for sand? No! To *bury your head in the sand* means to try and hide from a problem or to pretend there is no problem.

When kids are at the beach they sometimes bury each other in sand. First, their feet, then their legs, stomachs, chests, and arms. Then they stop. They bury everything except their heads! There is one animal that does put its head down in the sand. It is the ostrich. But it is not trying to hide from its problems. It is trying to hear if another animal is coming its way. If an enemy is coming, the ostrich can run away at 40 m.p.h.!

Imagine that you know your room needs cleaning. It looks like a hurricane hit it! But you keep trying to tell your parents and yourself that you really like it that way. Finally your dad says, "Your room is a mess! Stop *burying your head in the sand*! Instead use it to figure out where to start cleaning!"

A FEATHER IN YOUR CAP

What would you do if your principal told you that winning first prize in the Science Fair was *a feather in your cap*? Would you run to see if there was a feather in your baseball cap? No! To have *a feather in your cap* means that you have done something to be proud of.

There was a time when people really would have feathers put in their caps for doing something good. Picture a knight dressed in shining armor, fighting bravely to defend his king's castle! After long hours of battle, the enemy surrenders! The kingdom is safe! The king honors the knight and places a beautiful feather in his helmet so that everyone knows he is a brave warrior.

Imagine that your mom is given an award for all the hours she has worked as a volunteer at your school. When she tells you, you hug her and say, "Mom, that's *a feather in your cap!*"

ON THE NOSE

On the nose is an expression that means that someone did something exactly right! When a baseball player hits the ball *on the nose*, it goes flying into the outfield! When a pilot lands his airplane on the runway *on the nose*, the passengers are happy because he made a perfect landing and they are safely back down on the ground.

The phrase *on the nose* comes from people working at radio stations. When they want to tell the announcer something, they must silently give him signals. The signal for "You are doing great. The program is right on schedule!" is putting the finger *on the nose*.

Imagine that you are waiting for your best friend to come over to your house. She said that she would be there at 4 o'clock. Just as your clock strikes four, she rings your bell. You run to the door and say, "Hi, you're here right *on the nose!*"

LIKE A BULL IN A CHINA SHOP

What do you think would happen if a big clumsy bull were brought into a china shop full of beautiful dishes and let loose? You are right! CRASH! BOOM! BANG! Soon all the dishes would be broken! This probably never really happened, but we use this phrase when a rough or clumsy person says or does something that ruins everyone else's plans. We say that person is *like a bull in a china shop.*

Imagine that you are trying to talk your mom into letting you have water balloons at your birthday party. Suddenly your brother, Sam, comes in *like a bull in a china shop* and says he can't wait to hit everyone with the balloons. You can tell by the look on your mother's face that Sam has ruined any chance you may have had of convincing her.

BURY THE HATCHET

If someone says, "Let's *bury the hatchet*," it means that he or she wants to forget about a disagreement the two of you have had.

When one American Indian tribe would have a war with another tribe, they fought with clubs, bows and arrows, knives, and hatchets. When the war was over, both sides came together to make peace. They dug holes and buried their weapons to show that they would not fight anymore.

Imagine that you and a friend have been angry with each other for a week. You won't play together. You're both very unhappy. Finally you go to your friend and say, "Come on. Let's *bury the hatchet*! I want to be your friend again!"

A CHIP ON HIS SHOULDER

In Abraham Lincoln's day, boys who were angry had an unusual way of starting a fight. A boy would put a chip of wood on his shoulder and dare another boy to knock it off. Both boys knew that after the chip was knocked off, they were sure to fight each other. *A chip on your shoulder* was an invitation to fight!

Today we say someone has *a chip on his shoulder* when he acts unhappy, not in a sad way, but in an angry way, as if he wants to have a fight or an argument. Even when other people are nice to someone like that, he is hard to get along with.

Imagine that you were reading a book about a grouchy old dinosaur who always seemed to be looking for a fight. You could say, "Boy, he sure has *a chip on his shoulder*!"

TIP OF THE ICEBERG

If someone says, "Oh! That's just the *tip of the iceberg*!" he or she means that there is a much bigger problem than you can see.

An iceberg is an ice mountain that was once part of a glacier. After the iceberg breaks off from the glacier, it floats into the ocean. If an iceberg was only what you see above water, it wouldn't cause any problems. But under the water, an iceberg can be ten times bigger than what you see on top and it can be very dangerous if a ship hits it.

Imagine that one day your bike has a flat tire and you cut your finger while fixing the tire. You spill your milk on the rug. Your cat runs off and you can't find your favorite toy. When you see your friend, he says, "Oh, you have a little cut on your finger!" You could say, "That's just the *tip of the iceberg*!"

PULL THE WOOL OVER SOMEONE'S EYES

Have you ever noticed that George Washington is always pictured wearing a white wig? In Washington's day all the men who could afford those fancy wigs wore them. The wigs were made of "wool", as hair was called at one time. For people who wanted to trick or rob the gentlemen, the wigs were great! A thief would surprise the wig wearer by sneaking up behind him and pushing the wig down over his eyes so he could not see what the thief was going to do!

Today we say we *pull the wool over people's eyes* when we try to trick them into believing something that isn't true. Someone who tries to make his or her teacher think he or she completed the homework when he hadn't is trying to *pull the wool over the teacher's eyes.*

Imagine that you are watching a movie about a bank robber who moves to a new town and gets a job at a bank. You exclaim, "He sure *pulled the wool over their eyes!*"

GIVE HIM THE COLD SHOULDER

In the days of chivalry when knights wore shining armor, the brave knights knew they could always get a delicious hot meal at the end of the day in any home in the kingdom. People always prepared extra meat in the hope that a knight might honor them by coming to their house to eat and rest. Slowly the custom changed and people didn't want unexpected guests for dinner. The knights, who were no longer welcomed, would be given cold leftovers instead of the warm, roasted shoulder of lamb they used to enjoy. From those days came the saying to *give him the cold shoulder.* It means to pay no attention to someone so that he will go away!

Imagine that you and your sister see someone she used to date at the candy store. She makes believe she doesn't see him. You could say to your sister, "Boy, you really *gave him the cold shoulder!*"

TO GET UP ON THE WRONG SIDE OF THE BED

Have you ever had a bad day? A day when nothing seems to go right? Your mom might say, "You must have *gotten up on the wrong side of the bed!*" You wonder what she means—especially if your bed is against the wall!

Long ago, people thought that the left side of anything was unlucky, so if you got out of the bed on the left side, or put your left foot down first, you'd be in for a bad day. Some people put their beds against a wall just to be sure they never *get up on the wrong side of the bed!*

Imagine that on your way to school you drop your homework. Just as you go to pick it up the wind catches it and blows it over a fence into the park. Just as you come around the fence, you see your homework being chewed up by a lawn mower. You turn to your friends and say, "This morning, I must have *gotten up on the wrong side of the bed!*"

BLOW YOUR TOP

What do you think happens when you *blow your top*? Do you need a doctor to sew your head back on? No!! To *blow your top* means you're so angry that you lose control of your temper.

You'll understand why people say you *blow your top* if you think about how a volcano erupts. A mountain can look fine on the outside even when rumbling has started on the inside. Then suddenly there's a loud explosion, the top of the mountain seems to blow off and red hot lava flows out.

Imagine that a worker has been putting a new sidewalk in front of your house. He has spent all morning smoothing the concrete so it looks just right. As he puts his last tools away, a neighbor's dog sees a cat and chases it right through the wet cement! When the worker sees the paw prints in the wet cement, he *blows his top*!

WHITE ELEPHANT

A lot of people who don't have any animals have *white elephants*! A *white elephant* is something that is usually big, or costs a lot of money, and is hard to get rid of when you don't want it anymore!

The kings of Siam used to give real white elephants to people they didn't like. The elephants were very special. But feeding them cost so much that anyone who got one usually spent all his money on elephant food and didn't have any left for himself or his family!

Imagine that your family is having a garage sale. You are excited because you can finally get rid of the giant stuffed owl your aunt gave you years ago. When the sale is over, and your owl is still there, you moan, "That's not an owl. It's a *white elephant*!"

A CLOSE SHAVE

You can have a *close shave* even if you don't have whiskers! If you were climbing a mountain and a big rock fell down right beside you, but didn't hit you, you had a *close shave*—a narrow escape from danger!

Do you know how barbers first learn to shave people? Today they might practice on oranges or balls. But in the seventeenth century it was said that, "Barbers first learn to shave by shaving fools!" Those truly were close shaves, or narrow escapes from danger!

Imagine that you and a friend are climbing a tree. You start to put your foot on a branch, but stop to check if it is strong enough to hold you. The branch snaps off and falls to the ground! You say, "That was a close shave!"

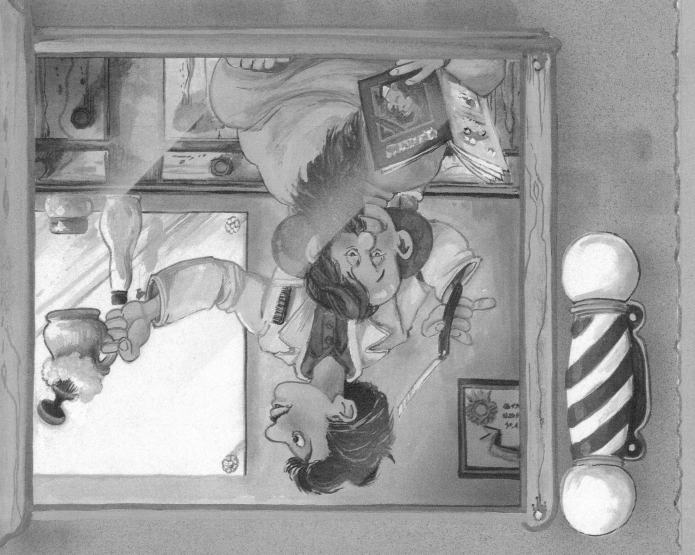

HAIR STANDING ON END

Cartoon artists show people who are very scared, by making their hair stick straight out! When you say, "That movie made my *hair stand on end*!" it means that you were very frightened!

Believe it or not, people have been saying this for thousands of years! The people who first said their *hair stood on end* were right! There are muscles at the bottom of our hairs. When we are scared these muscles tighten up and make our *hairs stand on end*!

Imagine that you are reading a book about the pirate Blackbeard. You shudder as you read about how he captured ships and threw the sailors overboard. You think, "Just reading about Blackbeard makes my *hair stand on end*!"

LET THE CAT OUT OF THE BAG

When you go to the grocery store, you choose your own bananas, milk, and hotdogs. They are put in a bag and you bring them home. Are you surprised when you open the bag at home? No, because you picked out everything yourself. But if you had lived over a 100 years ago and went to the market to buy a pig, there would be many people holding up bags calling, "Buy this pig!" If you were smart, you would look in the bag before you paid for it because sometimes the market people would trick unwise shoppers and put a cat in the bag instead of a pig! When the shopper got home, the cat would jump out of the bag and the shopper would realize he'd been tricked! The sellers had kept it a secret! But when the shopper got home and let the cat out of the bag, everyone knew the secret! Today we say "He let the cat out of the bag" when someone tells a secret!

Imagine that you are planning a surprise party for your grandfather. The day before the party, he calls to talk to your dad. You whisper to your dad, "Be sure you don't let the cat out of the bag about Grandpa's party!"

PUT A SOCK IN IT

If someone tells you to *put a sock in it*, don't run to your sock drawer! Instead, stop talking so much or so loudly!

There was a time when people really did use socks to quiet down noises. When Thomas Edison invented the phonograph, this wonderful machine could play music whenever you wanted to hear it. It had a big horn on it to make the sound louder, but there were no knobs to control how loud the music played. The only way to quiet the music was to put a sock in the horn. If it was still too loud, you would put two, three, or even four socks in the horn.

Imagine that the next time your sister's radio is too loud, you tell her to, *"Put a sock in it!"* But you'd better be ready to run, for she may throw a sock at you!

IN THE DOGHOUSE

People like to play with dogs and let them run around. But if a dog does something wrong, like chasing the mailman, it is sometimes tied up and put in its doghouse. This is a way of punishing the dog and making the mailman happy! Have you ever heard of a person being put *in the doghouse?* When a person misbehaves or causes trouble, he or she is said to be *in the doghouse.*

Imagine that you call your friend to see if he can go bike-riding with you. You are very surprised when he says, "Oh, I can't. I didn't clean my room and now I'm in the *doghouse* and my mom won't let me go out!"

BARKING UP THE WRONG TREE

Can you picture someone you know barking? That sounds silly doesn't it? But anyone could be told that he is *barking up the wrong tree*! Anyone who is trying to do something with the wrong person or in the wrong way is *barking up the wrong tree*! If the police are looking for a tall man, but it was a short man who broke the law, they are *barking up the wrong tree*!

This expression really did start with dogs—hunting dogs. In the days of Davey Crockett, a hunter took his dog out with him at night to hunt raccoons. When the raccoons heard the dog coming, they quickly climbed up a tree. The dog stood at the bottom of the tree and barked until the hunter got there. If the dog was *barking up the wrong tree*, the hunter went home without a raccoon.

Imagine that you have set up a scavenger hunt for your friends. You tell everyone that everything on the list is in your backyard. When you find one friend looking in the garage you say, "Sorry, Betty, but you're *barking up the wrong tree*!"

RINGS A BELL

When something sounds familiar, we say it *rings a bell*.

The "bell" in it *rings a bell* is like a doorbell. A doorbell has two parts: the button on the outside of the house and the bell that rings inside. The saying comes from the idea that when people tell us something we used to know, it is like they are pushing our doorbell button. The bell inside of our house—or head—rings when we start to remember what they are talking about.

Imagine that your brother is trying to get you to remember a scary movie that the two of you saw last year. "Remember there was a fire breathing dragon chasing a prince?" Even though you still can't remember the whole movie, this sounds familiar or *rings a bell*.

SAVED BY THE BELL

If you are *saved by the bell*, you have been rescued from danger or something unpleasant at just the right time! We say this when we think we have a problem and then just before it becomes serious something happens that we didn't expect and our troubles are over!

There are some people who really do hear a bell just in time! A boxer knows that he will hear a bell at the end of every round to tell him it's time to take a rest. If it rings just as he is about to be knocked out, the boxer really has been *saved by the bell*!

Imagine that your teacher is going around the room asking questions about something you forgot to study. You know you may soon be in trouble. Just before it's your turn, the bell rings for lunch! You were *saved by the bell*!

ONCE IN A BLUE MOON

If something happens *once in a blue moon*, it doesn't happen very often!

Has the moon ever been blue? Of course not! But sometimes something happens on earth that makes the moon look like it's blue. Once there was a huge forest fire in Canada that sent dust and sulphur high into the air. When people in England—a long way away—looked up, they saw a blue moon! It was really the moonlight shining through the dust!

Imagine that your team is playing soccer against the best team in town. The ball comes to you. The goal is far away. You kick the ball with all your might. It goes right through everyone's feet and into the net! You've scored the winning point! Later, you're telling your family about it and you say, "A kick like that happens *once in a blue moon!*"

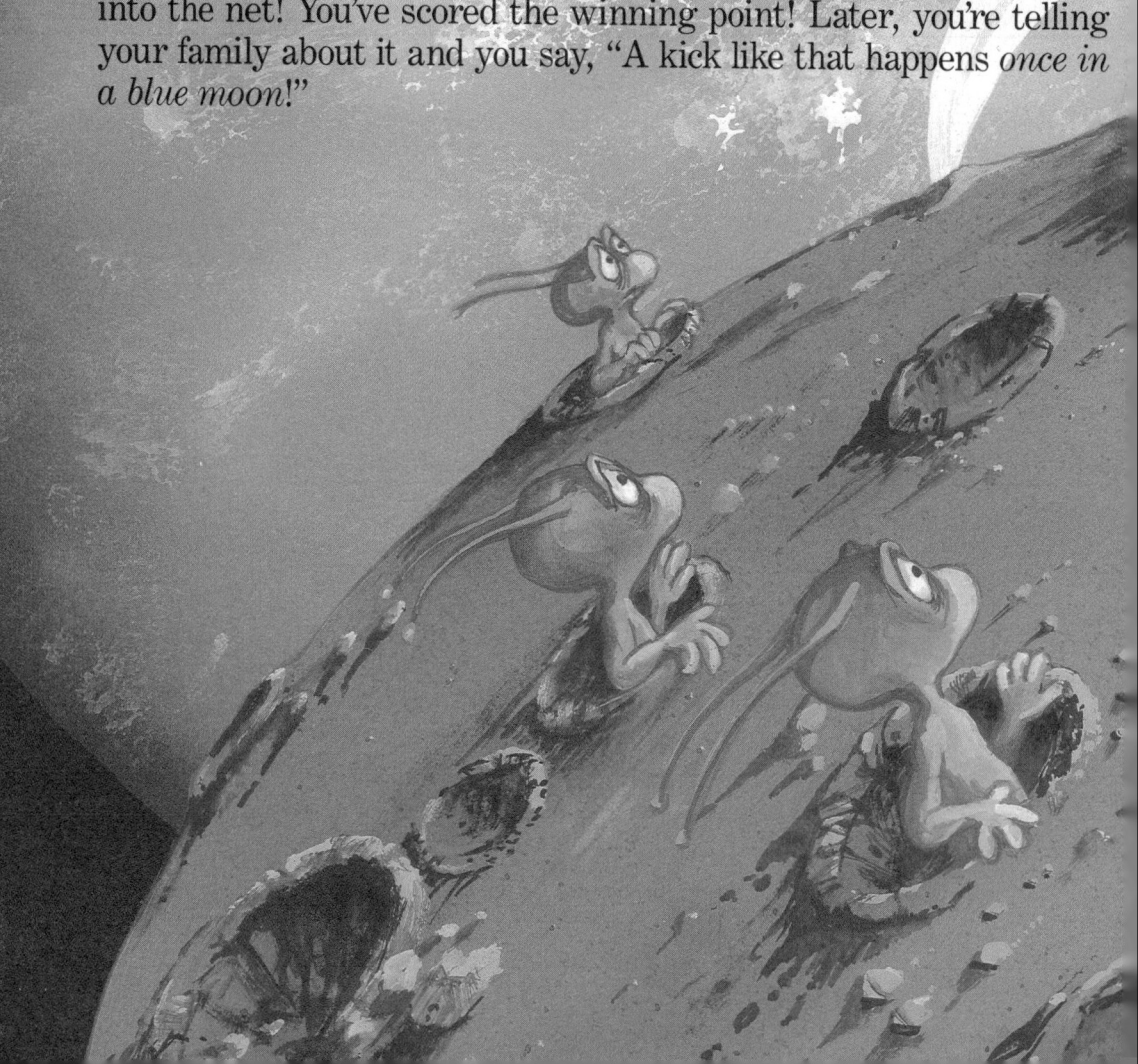

IN A PICKLE

Can you imagine someone being *in a pickle*? If you take a look at a pickle, you'd probably think there's no way you could ever be in one. But chances are that you have been *in a pickle* many times! Have you ever lost your lunchbox or broken something that wasn't yours? If you have ever been in any kind of trouble, you have been *in a pickle*!

Pickles are made by putting small cucumbers in water and salt for a long time. This salt water mixture used to be called a "pickle." If you sat *"in a pickle"* for a long time, you would be very uncomfortable—just as you are when you get in trouble!

Imagine that you borrowed your friend's new baseball to practice hitting. The first time you hit the ball, it flies over the fence and into a pond! You could say, "I'm really *in a pickle* now!"